MW01536900

# Little C,

# Praying God's
# **WISDOM**
# for Myself

Prayers and Fun Activities
Encouraging Children to Pray

## Hope McCardy
with **Lisa Bastian** and BROOKE & LEE

Illustrated by Stevie Burrows

Little Hands Praying God's WISDOM for Myself
Copyright © 2018 by Hope McCardy and
Color Me Reading Publishers

Scriptures quoted from the International Children's Bible ®, copyright ©1986, 1988, 1999, 2015 by Tommy Nelson. Used by permission.

For more information, or to enter our coloring competition, please email us or visit our websites:

**info@brookeandlee.com**
**www.brookeandlee.com**
**www.empoweringyourhope.com**

ISBN-13: 978-0-9976331-4-6
ISBN-10: 0-9976331-4-X

Printed in the United States of America.

# CONTENTS

COLOR ME
Reading

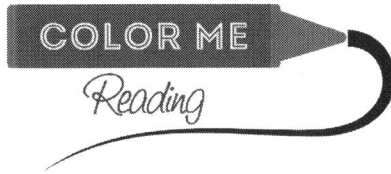

# Little Hands
# Praying God's WISDOM for Myself
# Formula:

Reading Content: 100%

Coloring Content: 48%

Activity Content: 15%

A little bit to color,
A little more to read.
A little bit of courage,
As we aim to plant a seed.


Through colors and writing,
Through moments we share.
To be creative and inviting,
For children everywhere.


Learning we expect,
But fun we require.
The only rule we accept,
Is to *believe, imagine, and inspire.*


BROOKE LEE

# Get on the WISDOM Wagon Song

(Repeat 2X)
Get on the WISDOM Wagon
Get on the WISDOM Wagon
Get on the WISDOM Wagon
Get on it! Get on it!

Chorus
Get on the WISDOM Wagon
We won't leave without you
So glad to have you join us
We welcome you, we do.

Verse
**W** is for **WISE**
**I** is for **INSIGHTFUL**
**S** is for a **SENSITIVE** heart
For which, we are so thankful.
**D** is for **DISCERNING**
**O** is for **OBEDIENT**
**M** is for **MOTIVATED**
An extra special ingredient.

Chorus
Get on the WISDOM Wagon
We won't leave without you
So glad to have you join us
We welcome you, we do.

(Repeat 2X)
Get on the WISDOM Wagon
Get on the WISDOM Wagon
Get on the WISDOM Wagon
Get on it! Get on it!

# Get on the WISDOM Wagon!
## With

Matt    Rae    Lee    Aif

WISDOM Wagon

and friends!

W is for WISE
I is for INSIGHTFUL
S is for SENSITIVE
D is for DISCERNING
O is for OBEDIENT
M is for MOTIVATED

2

# W is for WISE

## WISDOM Wagon Prayers

1. HELP ME TO BE UNDERSTANDING
2. MAKE ME WISE

# HELP ME TO BE UNDERSTANDING

## WISDOM Wagon Bible Verse

*...Make understanding your closest friend.* - **Proverbs 7:4b**

## Little Hands Praying for Myself

Father, help me to be understanding,
Even though I am only a youth.
I know there is so much for me to learn,
So Father, please show me the truth.

Lead me and direct me daily, I pray;
Help me to love following You.
Show me just how to make the wise choices
In all that I think, say, and do.

Teach me, so I know the time to say "Yes;"
Make me strong: so I can say "No."
Turn my heart toward Your awesome wisdom;
Point my eyes to see where You go.

Father, help me to be understanding.
In Jesus' name. Amen.

# W is for WISE

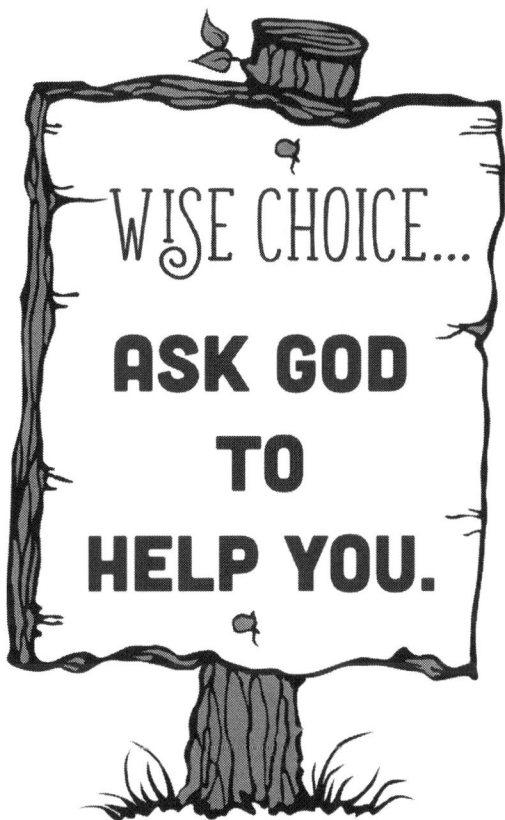

WISE CHOICE...

**ASK GOD TO HELP YOU.**

## SELF-TALK: WORDS I TELL MYSELF

Little Hands, say these words out loud!
**With Father God's help, I will be more understanding.**

# MAKE ME WISE

## WISDOM Wagon Bible Verse

*The wise person is rewarded by his wisdom.* - **Proverbs 9:12a**

### Little Hands Praying for Myself

Lord, make me wise today and every day;
Help me to see what You want me to see.
Turn me away from my own selfish way,
So I can be all You want me to be.

Where I am rather strong, give me Your grace;
Where I am so weak, kindly show me Your Face.

Help me choose wisdom each day of my life,
And please, loving Lord, keep me away from strife.

Lord, make me wise today and every day.
In Jesus' name. Amen.

# W is for WISE

## SELF-TALK: WORDS I TELL MYSELF

Little Hands, say these words out loud!
**With the Lord's anointing, I will become wise.**

# WISDOM Wagon Activities

## W is for WISE

**Word Challenge:** Give three synonyms (words with similar meanings) for the WISDOM word, **wise**. The first one is provided for you.

**Wise**: intelligent, _____, and _____

## Think About It

What wise choices will you make today?

1) _____

2) _____

3) _____

## Put Into Practice

- Try very hard **not** to gossip. I know this is extremely hard to do. **Ask God to help you, okay?**
- For the next 24 hours, I challenge you: **Do not say anything negative (bad) about anybody.** Jesus will assist you if you ask Him to.

# I is for INSIGHTFUL

## WISDOM Wagon Prayers

3. TEACH ME TO ASK GOOD QUESTIONS
4. SHOW ME HOW TO BE RESPECTFUL

# TEACH ME TO ASK GOOD QUESTIONS

## WISDOM Wagon Bible Verse

*But if any of you needs wisdom, you should ask God for it.*
- James 1:5a

## Little Hands Praying for Myself

*D*ear God, teach me to ask good questions;
Please lead me to where You want me to go.
Show me the best people to talk to
When there is something that I want to know.

Help me to look for godly insight,
And be sure to follow where it may lead.
Most of all, I look to You, Dear Lord;
I look to You for the wisdom I need.

Dear God, teach me to ask good questions.
In Jesus' name. Amen.

# I is for INSIGHTFUL

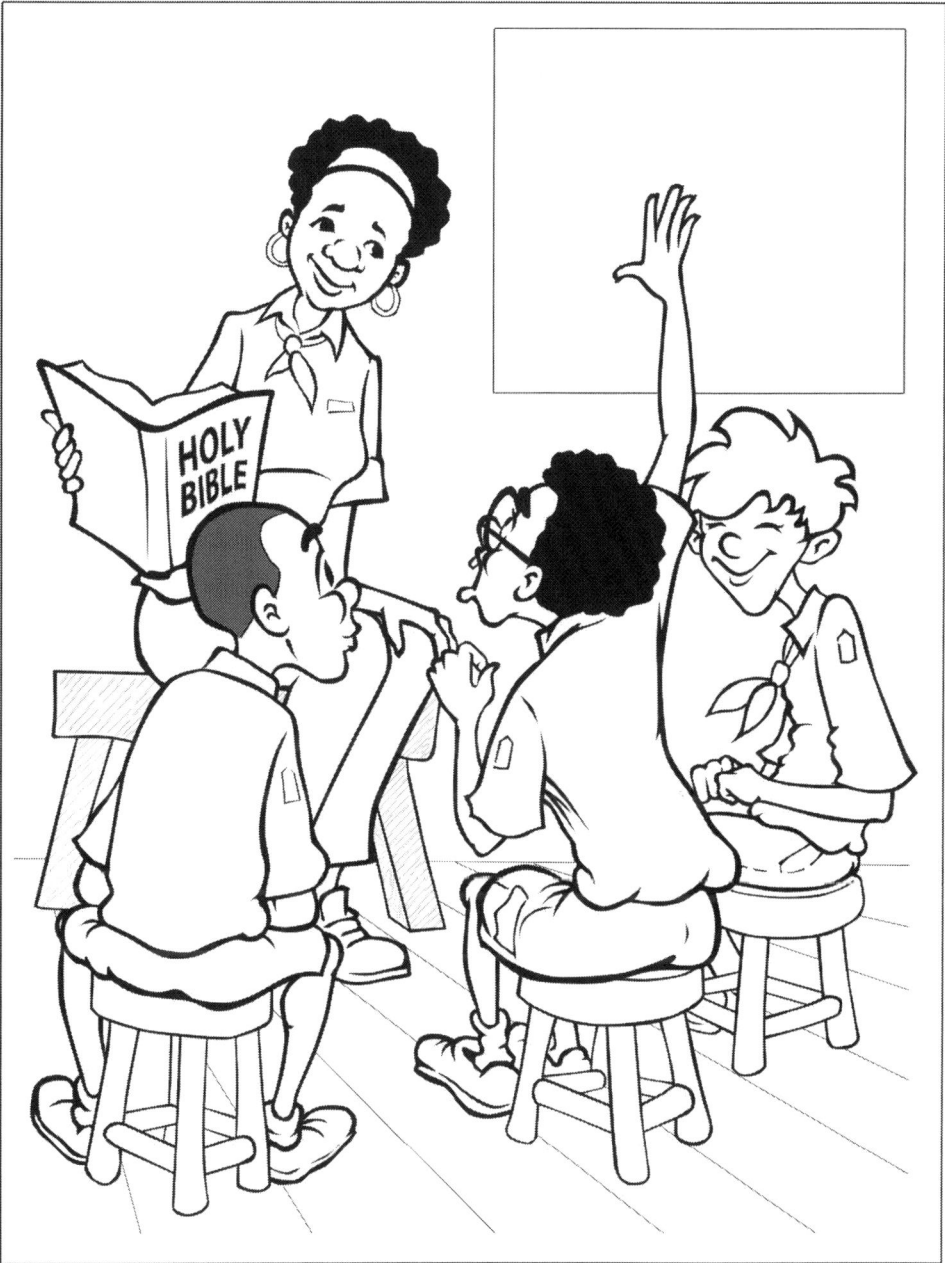

## SELF-TALK: WORDS I TELL MYSELF

Little Hands, say these words out loud!

**With God's insight, I will learn to ask good questions.**

# SHOW ME HOW TO BE RESPECTFUL

## WISDOM Wagon Bible Verse

*Knowledge begins with respect for the Lord.* - **Proverbs 1:7a**

## Little Hands Praying for Myself

*H*eavenly Father, show me how to be respectful;
Teach me genuine respect for You.
Help me, every day, to love and respect my parents
In the true way that You want me to.

Fill me to the brim with self-respect and real wisdom;
Give me insight, to look up to You.
Encourage me to respect each and every teacher
And all those in authority, too.

When it is indeed challenging to respect my friends,
Help me to remember how much You care.
Put Your tender love and thoughtful concern in my
    heart;
And may You teach me how to be fair.

Heavenly Father, show me how to be respectful.
In Jesus' name. Amen.

# I is for INSIGHTFUL

## SELF-TALK: WORDS I TELL MYSELF

Little Hands, say these words out loud!
**With My Heavenly Father's guiding hand,
I will learn how to be respectful.**

# WISDOM Wagon Activities

## I is for INSIGHTFUL

**Word Challenge:** Give three synonyms (words with similar meanings) for the WISDOM word, **insightful**. The first one is provided for you.

**Insightful**: keen, _____, and _____

## Think About It

Who would you ask for assistance in the following situations?

a) If you were lost _____

b) If you were sick _____

c) If you were sad _____

d) If you were angry _____

## Put Into Practice

- **Respect God and ask Him for wisdom every day!**

# S is for SENSITIVE

## WISDOM Wagon Prayers

5. GUIDE MY THOUGHTS
6. MAKE ME CAREFUL IN WHAT I SAY

# GUIDE MY THOUGHTS

## WISDOM Wagon Bible Verse

*Be very careful about what you think. Your thoughts run your life.*
**- Proverbs 4:23**

## Little Hands Praying for Myself

Father God, please guide my thoughts, I pray,
Because they decide my actions.
Make me sensitive to what I hear,
And keep me from all distractions.

Give me the desire to think good thoughts
Of myself, and those around me:
Thoughts that Jesus would like me to think,
Leading me to live more wisely.

Father God, please guide my thoughts, I pray.
In Jesus' name. Amen.

# S is for SENSITIVE

## SELF-TALK: WORDS I TELL MYSELF

Little Hands, say these words out loud!
**With Father God's sensitivity, I will guide my thoughts.**

# MAKE ME CAREFUL IN THE WORDS I SAY

## WISDOM Wagon Bible Verse

*...Watch what you say.* - **Proverbs 5:2b**

## Little Hands Praying for Myself

*D*ear Jesus, make me careful in the words I say;
Help me to watch my mouth very closely, I pray.

Keep me aware of the hurt careless words can cause;
When I am so angry, encourage me to pause.

Teach me how to listen and pray before I speak;
Help me to be an example to those who are weak.

Dear Jesus, make me careful in the words I say.
In Your name, I pray. Amen.

# S is for SENSITIVE

## SELF-TALK: WORDS I TELL MYSELF

Little Hands, say these words out loud!
**With Jesus' thoughtfulness,
I will be careful in the words I say.**

# WISDOM Wagon Activities

## S is for SENSITIVE

**Word Challenge:** Give three synonyms (words with similar meanings) for the WISDOM word, **sensitive**. The first one is provided for you.

Sensitive: delicate, _____ , and _____

### Think About It

1. Do you often think bad thoughts?  When you do, do you follow those thoughts?

   _____

2. Do you sometimes tend to talk too much?  If so, when?

   _____

### Put Into Practice

- Bad thoughts??? **Think about JESUS.**  He turns a frown upside down.  →

- (2 ears) + (1 mouth) = **Listen two times (double) as much as you talk.  Ask God to help you, okay?**

# D is for DISCERNING

## WISDOM Wagon Prayers

7. INSPIRE ME TO BEHAVE
8. HELP ME TO CHOOSE FRIENDS WISELY

# INSPIRE ME TO BEHAVE

## WISDOM Wagon Bible Verse

*The mind of a smart person is ready to get knowledge. The wise person listens to learn more.* - **Proverbs 18:15**

## Little Hands Praying for Myself

Father, inspire me to behave myself every day;
Show me how far I can go.
Bless me with fitting discernment and good common
    sense;
Teach me the things I should know.

Help me to put up the needed boundaries in my life;
Anoint me with self-control.
Give me strong desire to read Your Word day by day;
Make me courageous and bold.

Father, inspire me to behave myself every day.
In Jesus' name. Amen.

# D is for DISCERNING

Even if you
are the only
ONE –

DO
WHAT
IS RIGHT!

## SELF-TALK: WORDS I TELL MYSELF

Little Hands, say these words out loud!
**With Father God's guidance, I am inspired to behave myself.**

# HELP ME TO CHOOSE FRIENDS WISELY

## WISDOM Wagon Bible Verse

*Whoever spends time with wise people will become wise.*
- Proverbs 13:20a

## Little Hands Praying for Myself

Lord, help me to choose my friends wisely;
Show me the kids I should hang around.
Push me to pick my pals carefully,
Friends with character – godly and sound.

May my friends decide to do good deeds,
Loving You and other personnel.
May they know You supply all their needs,
And some of their desires as well.

Lord, help me to choose my friends wisely.
In Jesus' name. Amen.

# D is for DISCERNING

## SELF-TALK: WORDS I TELL MYSELF

Little Hands, say these words out loud!
**With the Lord's discernment to lead me,
I will choose my friends wisely.**

# WISDOM Wagon Activities

## D is for DISCERNING

**Word Challenge:** Give three synonyms (words with similar meanings) for the WISDOM word, **discerning**. The first one is provided for you.

**Discerning**:  sharp, _____ , and _____

**Think About It:**  What kind of people do you often hang around?  Circle your answer(s).  You can have more than one answer if you would like.

| | |
|---|---|
| Happy persons | Naughty persons |
| Sad people | Diligent guys and girls |
| Grumpy individuals | Wise people |
| Smart people | Silly folks |
| Helpful folks | Rude persons |

## Put Into Practice

- **Be smart** and **choose your friends wisely!**

# O is for OBEDIENT

## WISDOM Wagon Prayers

9. TEACH ME TO LISTEN TO MY PARENTS
10. HELP ME TO RECEIVE CORRECTION

# TEACH ME TO LISTEN TO MY PARENTS

## WISDOM Wagon Bible Verse

*Children, obey your parents the way the Lord wants. This is the right thing to do.* - **Ephesians 6:1**

## Little Hands Praying for Myself

God, teach me to listen to my parents,
As they demonstrate right from wrong.
I ask for Your blessings to make me smart,
So I grow to be wise and strong.

Fill mommy and daddy with great wisdom;
May they strive to encourage me.
Inspire me to obey their wise advice,
And instructions diligently.

Although growing up can be really tough
On both the parent and the child,
Bless us, dear Father, please bless us indeed;
Make obedience all worthwhile.

God, teach me to listen to my parents.
In Jesus' name. Amen.

# O is for OBEDIENT

## SELF-TALK: WORDS I TELL MYSELF

Little Hands, say these words out loud!
**With God's command to be obedient,
I will listen to my parents.**

# HELP ME TO RECEIVE CORRECTION

## WISDOM Wagon Bible Verse

*Listen to advice and accept correction. Then in the end you will be wise.* - **Proverbs 19:20**

## Little Hands Praying for Myself

*D*ear God, help me to listen and receive correction
From those, You have placed over me.
My daddy and mommy, teachers, and all others who
Discipline me regularly.

May I not shout out such loud disagreeable words
Or shed big fat crocodile tears.
But instead, may I select to obedient be
And grow wise in my younger years.

Dear God, help me to listen and receive correction.
In Jesus' name. Amen.

# O is for OBEDIENT

## SELF-TALK: WORDS I TELL MYSELF

Little Hands, say these words out loud!
**With God's courage and power,
I will receive the correction I need.**

# WISDOM Wagon Activities

## O is for OBEDIENT

**Word Challenge:** Give three synonyms (words with similar meanings) for the WISDOM word, **obedient**. The first one is provided for you.

**Obedient**: respectful, _____, and _____

**Think About It:** Your mother tells you to clean your room, but instead you decide to play a video game.

1. How do you think your mom would feel?

   _____

   _____

2. How do you think God feels?

   _____

   _____

## Put Into Practice

- Receiving correction can be quite difficult at times. It can make you feel a bit sad (or even angry). The next time someone tries to correct you, **don't jump to defend yourself. Take time to think about what they are saying.** (You can do this with the Lord's help. I know you can!)

# M is for MOTIVATED

## WISDOM Wagon Prayers

11. PUSH ME NOT TO BE LAZY
12. SHOW ME HOW TO LOVE OTHERS

# PUSH ME NOT TO BE LAZY

## WISDOM Wagon Bible Verse

*The person who works his land will have plenty of food.*
**- Proverbs 12:11a**

### Little Hands Praying for Myself

Heavenly Father, push me not to be lazy;
Make me see the value of hard work.
Motivate me, so I desire to be useful;
Help me not to respond like a jerk.

May nothing be too tiny or too enormous,
For my eager little hands to do.
Anoint me with Your great wisdom overflowing;
So I perform my chores to please You.

Heavenly Father, push me not to be lazy.
In Jesus' name. Amen.

# M is for MOTIVATED

## SELF-TALK: WORDS I TELL MYSELF

Little Hands, say these words out loud!

**With my Heavenly Father's push and motivation,
I will not be lazy.**

# SHOW ME HOW TO LOVE OTHERS

## WISDOM Wagon Bible Verse

*Do for other people what you want them to do for you.* - **Luke 6:31**

### Little Hands Praying for Myself

Jesus, show me how I ought to love others
In the way You have shown love to me.
Help me to care for my sisters and brothers;
Push me to forgive, liberally.

Sprinkle my heart with gentle understanding,
So my words bring joy to all who hear.
May I be kind and not over-demanding;
Dear Jesus, please do keep, ever near.

As God has been gracious and loving to me,
Help me to seek, always, to please You.
Remove all sin from my heart and set it free;
Make me love You in all that I do.

Jesus, show me how I ought to love others.
In Your name, I pray. Amen.

# M is for MOTIVATED

## SELF-TALK: WORDS I TELL MYSELF

Little Hands, say these words out loud!

**With Jesus' inspiration and assistance,
I will learn how to love others.**

# WISDOM Wagon Activities

## M is for MOTIVATED

**Word Challenge:** Give three synonyms (words with similar meanings) for the WISDOM word, **motivated**. The first one is provided for you.

   **Motivated:** inspired, _____, and _____

### Think About It

1. Are you a helpful child?  List some of the things you do to help your teachers.

   _____

   _____

2. What can you do at home this week to help or serve your family?

   _____

   _____

### Put Into Practice

- When you see dirty dishes in the sink, **wash them without having to be told to do so.**
- To serve or help is a way to show love.  **Perform a special act of service for someone this week.**

**Get on the WISDOM Wagon!**
Choose to Pray for **WISDOM** Daily!

# Summary

## Review of SELF-TALK: WORDS I TELL MYSELF

# W is for WISE

- With Father God's help, I will be more understanding.
- With the Lord's anointing, I will become wise.

# I is for INSIGHTFUL

- With God's insight, I will learn to ask good questions.
- With my Heavenly Father's guiding hand, I will learn how to be respectful.

# S is for SENSITIVE

- With Father God's sensitivity, I will guide my thoughts.
- With Jesus' thoughtfulness, I will be careful in the words I say.

# D is for DISCERNING

- With Father God's guidance, I am inspired to behave myself.
- With the Lord's discernment to lead me, I will choose my friends wisely.

# O is for OBEDIENT

- With God's command to be obedient, I will listen to my parents.
- With God's courage and power, I will receive the correction I need.

# M is for MOTIVATED

- With my Heavenly Father's push and motivation, I will not be lazy.
- With Jesus' inspiration and assistance, I will learn how to love others.

# Other COLOR ME Reading Titles Available

- ☺ Little Hands Praying God's WISDOM for My Family
- ☺ Little Hands Praying God's WISDOM for My Friends
- ☺ Dave the Brave
- ☺ Mr. Friend
- ☺ Crayons and Colors

Go to
www.brookeandlee.com
to visit our site, listen to our songs,
and to join the coloring competition for
*Little Hands Praying God's WISDOM for Myself!*

Made in the USA
Las Vegas, NV
18 November 2021

34729620R00026